Acclaim for

JONATHAN RABAN's

Old Glory

"He can skewer life in an anecdote and evoke a river scene in a few brushstrokes." —*The Nation*

"Wonderful. . . . Mr. Raban . . . is excellent company. He is a popcorn-popper of opinions, and they are unpredictable."
—*The New York Times Book Review*

"Mr. Raban has a keen ear, but for the river itself, he has to evince not only a keen eye but a capacity to use a painter's palette. He gives us the strong brown god in all its rage, sullenness and beauty." —Anthony Burgess

"Throughout his epic journey he struggles to reconcile the real, treacherous, protean river with the shimmering dream-waters of his boyhood. This is what gives his book its remarkable power, elevating it close to the level of myth."
—Salman Rushdie

JONATHAN RABAN

Old Glory

Jonathan Raban is the author of *Soft City, Arabia, Foreign Land, Coasting, For Love and Money, Hunting Mr. Heartbreak,* and the bestselling *Bad Land,* winner of the National Book Critics Circle Award. He won the W.H. Heinemann Award for Literature in 1982 and the Thomas Cook Award in 1981 and 1991. He also edited *The Oxford Book of the Sea.* He lives in Seattle.